Welcome

NAOMI STARKEY

There is something about water that captures our imagination, in the UK at least! Maybe it is something to do with living on an island. Websites devoted to selling waterside property show the premium placed on something with a sea/river/lake view, if only a rather rickety boat on a cramped canal mooring. Even if we don't live by water, we may love sailing, swimming, surfing or simply walking by it.

As a number of the articles in this issue mention, water is inescapably—and obviously—a global issue. So often taken for granted in relatively cool and rainy northern countries, access to water (or the lack of it) is literally a matter of life or death for far too many people around the world. Ours is a blue planet, almost wholly water when seen from space, but we squander this precious resource at our peril.

In the Bible, water is a dominant image used to express something of God's blessing and also his transforming power. From 'creation to re-creation' (in the words of Jo Bailey Wells), from Genesis to Revelation, this most evocative of symbols speaks to us of our maker and redeemer, and demonstrates his unfailing love and care for us. When we thirst, he offers us the living water that truly satisfies, and in the waters of baptism we see a reminder of his saving love, bringing us from death to eternal life.

Naomi Starkey

This compilation copyright © BRF 2007
Authors retain copyright in their own work
Illustrations copyright © Ray and Corinne Burrows, Chris Daunt and Ian Mitchell 2007

**Published by
The Bible Reading Fellowship**
First Floor, Elsfield Hall
15–17 Elsfield Way, Oxford OX2 8FG
Websites: www.brf.org.uk and www.quietspaces.org.uk
ISBN 978 1 84101 499 9
First published 2007
10 9 8 7 6 5 4 3 2 1 0
All rights reserved

Acknowledgments
Scripture quotations taken from The New Revised Standard Version of the Bible, Anglicized Edition, copyright © 1989, 1995 by the Division of Christian Education of the National Council of the Churches of Christ in the USA, are used by permission. All rights reserved.

Scripture quotations taken from the Holy Bible, New International Version, copyright © 1973, 1978, 1984 by International Bible Society, are used by permission of Hodder & Stoughton, a division of Hodder Headline Ltd. All rights reserved. 'NIV' is a registered trademark of International Bible Society. UK trademark number 1448790.

Scriptures quoted from the Good News Bible published by The Bible Societies/HarperCollins Publishers Ltd, UK © American Bible Society 1966, 1971, 1976, 1992, used with permission.

Scripture quotations marked ESV are from The Holy Bible, English Standard Version, published by HarperCollins Publishers © 2001 Crossway Bibles, a division of Good News Publishers. Used by permission. All rights reserved.

A catalogue record for this book is available from the British Library

Printed by Gutenberg Press, Tarxien, Malta

Quiet Spaces

CONTENTS

Irrepressible blessing, heavenly overwhelming 4
Jo Bailey Wells

Drinking water and living water 11
David Douglas

Orders for an anchoress 17
Veronica Zundel

Water—God's gift...........................18
Joyce Huggett

Reflections from a Christian surfer ..24
Michael Volland

The Community of Aidan and Hilda and the Holy Island of Lindisfarne....28
Ray Simpson

Wash and flood 33
Nigel Holmes

Ministering angels 37
Carol Hathorne

Music for the soul: Many waters cannot quench Love........................38
Gordon Giles

The hidden life of the oyster............41
Emma Garrow

At the well of healing......................44
Anne Hibbert

John Newton's life of amazing grace 50
Jean Watson

The seawater kingdom 53
Naomi Starkey

Prayer through the week..................59
Tony Horsfall

Musings of a middle-aged mystic 61
Veronica Zundel

Irrepressible blessing, heavenly overwhelming

Jo Bailey Wells is Director of Anglican Studies at Duke Divinity School in North Carolina, USA, having moved from the UK in 2005. She teaches, she writes, she talks, she travels and is amazed that some call this 'work'—given how much harder are the domestic challenges of young children.

'Water, water everywhere'

Images of water stream through the scriptures from beginning to end. It is watery chaos that undergirds creation: the wind of God's Spirit makes waves and an orderly pattern emerges as the cosmic ocean recedes. Except at the flood, God keeps the tide of these waters in check in order to enable the space for life to unfurl. It is through channelled rivers, neatly branching into streams, that the garden of Eden (Genesis 2:6, 10)—indeed, all of creation—is irrigated to be the nourishing and flourishing stage upon which each living thing finds its place.

The temple, the very locus and focus of God's dwelling on earth, is depicted in a vision at the end of Ezekiel as having water springing up within it and flowing from it to form a far-reaching river that revives and refreshes 'every living creature, wherever the river goes' (Ezekiel 47:9). For example, on the banks of this river are found life-sustaining trees, whose fruit provides food and whose leaves offer healing (v. 12).

The book of Revelation develops the same linkage of the physical with the spiritual to depict God's new creation, where a life-sustaining flow of water is seen to stream from the throne of God and of the Lamb (22:1), thereby quenching the thirst of all (v. 17). The matter of water undergirds the whole biblical story of the world, from creation to re-creation, from Genesis to Revelation, across time and across the universe.

Source of life

I have recently returned from the country of Sudan. Much of this land—straddling North and East Africa, the largest in the whole continent of Africa—is desert. There is little that can grow naturally in such hot, dry conditions during most of the year. As the aeroplane circled over the capital city, Khartoum, built at the point where the White Nile and Blue Nile join forces as they head northwards towards Egypt, I realized as if for the first time how crucial water is for life. Rather like a coiling, colourful snake, the river shimmers with the blue of the water and the rich green of its banks, wending a winding path through vast expanses of seemingly empty, dry brown earth. Apart from the Nile, this region would be uninhabitable. Because of its life-sustaining flow, there are trees and crops, there is commerce and community, a hubbub of activity along its wide and fertile banks.

As if springing from a remote yet rich sanctuary of God—the Ruwenzori mountains of Uganda and the far highlands of Ethiopia—the waters of the Nile do not run dry. Nor do they stand still or become stagnant.

> It is watery chaos that undergirds creation

Rather, they sustain the very real needs of many tribes and nations, over thousands of miles, through to the delta region of northern Egypt where the Nile meets the Mediterranean Sea—and here the soil offers some of the richest growing conditions found anywhere in the world.

Threat to life

Much of the power of water imagery relies on the tension between abundance and scarcity. There is either too much or not enough.

In many underdeveloped parts of the world, both extremes are evidenced in seemingly alternating sequence, to devastating effect: either there is flood or there is drought. But the biblical narrative of creation (both the original creation and the new creation) is noted for its equilibrium. Unlike in some of the ancient Babylonian myths of creation, the water does not get out of hand: rather, God's perfect control is demonstrated throughout. The Genesis 1 narrative stresses order and design in a pattern of repetition and symmetry. Even at the flood—where there are further echoes of Babylonian texts—the biblical account underlines God's sovereignty throughout. God *decided* to send a flood, thus undoing some of his own work of creation, owing to the wickedness all around. Indeed, even though the heart of humanity had not changed (Genesis 8:21), God *rescinded* the flood and promised never again to destroy the earth in this way (9:11).

Such promises are universal and eternal in their scope. They may not feel as if they have an effect at a particular time and more local place.

> **God is not destroying creation; the water does not represent God's judgment**

God's grace and sovereignty in creation and re-creation—the picture of overflowing waters held back, of parched places watered—does not deny the reality of droughts or torrents within history. Before the end of Genesis there is a drought and famine in Egypt, through which circumstances Joseph ascends to high office under Pharaoh and God's providence is illustrated in surprising ways (50:20). Equally, in a world of tsunamis and Hurricane Katrinas, we may cling to the assurance of the one universal flood: God is not destroying creation; the water does not represent God's judgment.

Unlike many earthly rivers, God's 'universal' river does not run dry; it does not become stagnant; its waters may be trusted to cleanse and heal. Yet in the experience of people living in the biblical lands and in much of the world today, water is a scarce commodity: rivers carry infections, wells run dry. In the town where I stayed in Sudan, every drop that fell during the rainy season was collected from rooftops and stored. The rest of the year it was distributed by donkey cart and sold by the litre: water barely fit to cleanse, most unlikely to heal.

Symbol of salvation, sustenance, community, cleansing

Thus far we have discussed water in cosmic terms, as a primary material through which God's universal work of creation and re-creation is depicted

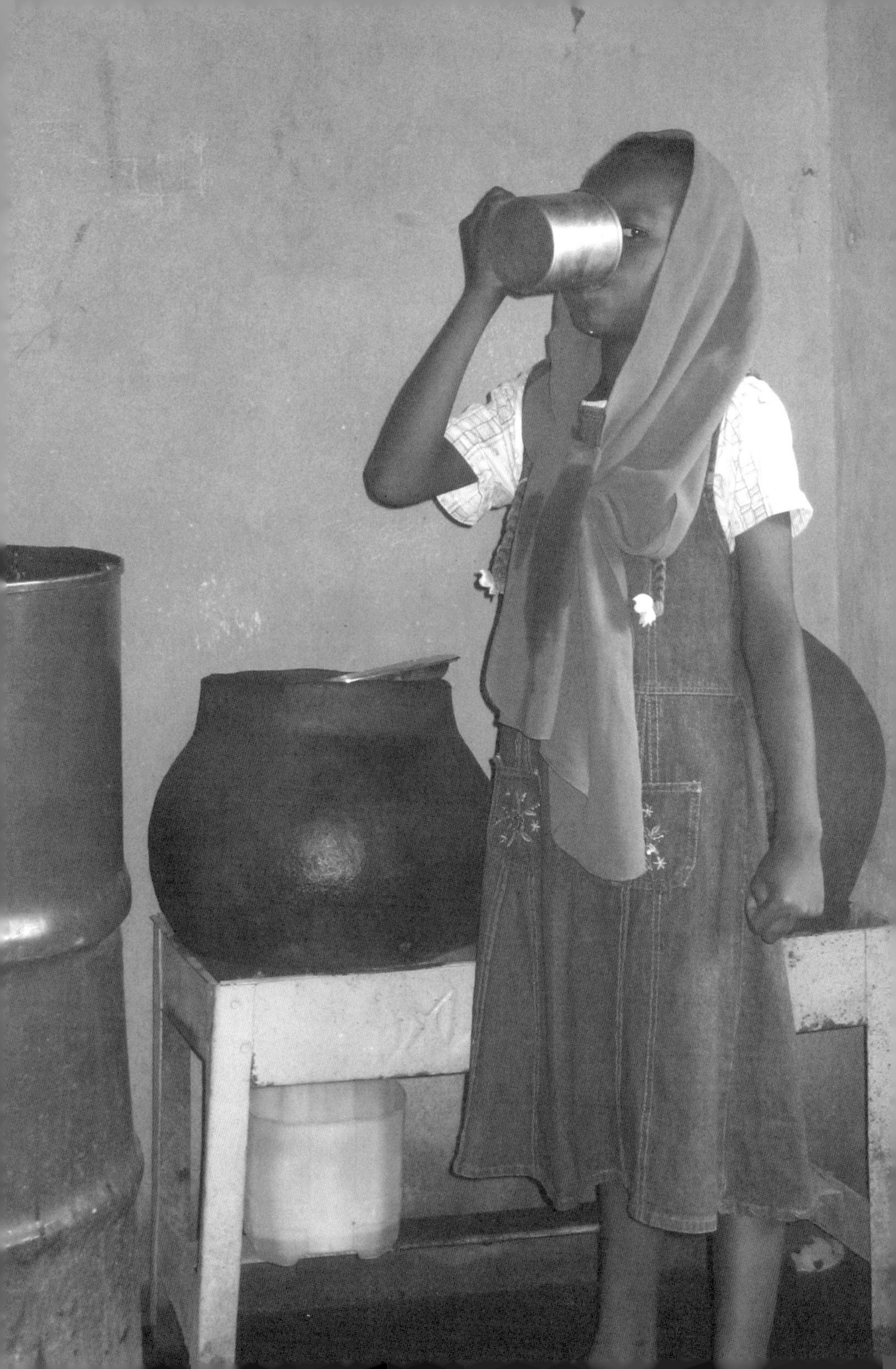

> **Water is a symbol of community, of conversation and conviviality**

The river shimmers with the blue of the water and the rich green of its banks

and communicated. Aside from these universals, water also plays a very important role in the particular account of God's people, in the salvation history that begins with the calling of Abraham and continues with the people of Israel, culminating in Jesus.

It is in the parting of the waters of the Red Sea that the Hebrew people come to understand God's extraordinary work of salvation. As the exodus from Egypt defines their salvation—their release from slavery and their formation as God's people—so the parting of the Red Sea defines the exodus. God is not only able to command the oceans universally, as at creation, but he can and does also command them to rescue his chosen people. When Jesus walks on water,

when the wind and waves obey him, Jesus is demonstrating his divinity and declaring the same power to save. So water becomes a symbol of salvation and spiritual birth.

In the wilderness, parched and desperate on their way to the promised land, God's people are given water to drink, flowing from a rock (Exodus 17:1–6). This gift of water comes to epitomize God's generous, even miraculous, provision in time of need (Isaiah 48:21). The promised land, the longed-for end of their desert journey, is 'a good land' because it is 'a land with flowing streams, with springs and underground waters welling up in valleys and hills' (Deuteronomy 8:7). Even in the 'normal' routines of rain and dew, God's provision is seen to continue enriching the land (Psalm 65:9–10), until, parched and exiled in another wilderness, the promise to lead the people beside springs of water is voiced again (Isaiah 49:10). Water is a symbol of blessing—whether still waters (Psalm 23:2) or overflowing springs (Malachi 3:10). This blessing is ultimately irrepressible.

Many of the daily routines of life in the biblical lands—as, for example, in Sudan today—centred around water. Towns were built beside rivers, villages sprang up around wells, and the source of water became a source of community. Thus the site of a well, typically, became the public plaza, a place to 'hang out', meet friends and enjoy company. It is no surprise, then, that it was through an encounter at a well, the focus of community, that Isaac found Rebekah (Genesis 24), Jacob found Rachel (Genesis 29), Moses found Zipporah (Exodus 2) and Jesus met the Samaritan woman (John 4). In this sense, water is a symbol of community, of conversation and conviviality—perhaps equivalent to a beach in summertime today.

When settled in the land, water plays an important ritual function in Israel. Just as with the washing rituals observed by the Pharisees during Jesus' day (Mark 7:3–4; John 2:6; 3:25), so various habits of ceremonial cleansing with water are prescribed or described among Old Testament laws, many in preparation for worship. 'A bronze basin for washing' is placed between the altar and the tent of meeting (Exodus 30:18) or the temple (2 Chronicles 4:6). Levites are consecrated for God's service by being sprinkled with water of cleansing (Numbers 8:7). The spoils of war are purified with water (31:23). This ceremonial aspect of water explains the prophet Ezekiel's announcement that in days to come the Lord God himself 'will sprinkle clean water' on the house of Israel (Ezekiel 36:25). The letter to the Ephesians describes how Christ loved the church enough 'to make her holy by cleansing her with the washing of water by the word' (Ephesians 5:26). Titus 3:5 puts it, 'He saved us… through the water of rebirth and renewal by the Holy Spirit.'

Water of baptism

All of these various associations with water, both in the universal story of God's creation and in the particular story of God's people, come together in the significance of the water of baptism. Notice the multiple symbolism in this prayer of blessing found in one example of a baptism liturgy, from *Common Worship*:

We thank you, almighty God, for the gift of water to sustain, refresh and cleanse all life. Over water the Holy Spirit moved in the beginning of creation. Through water you led the children of Israel from slavery in Egypt to freedom in the Promised Land. In water your Son Jesus received the baptism of John and was anointed by the Holy Spirit as the Messiah, the Christ, to lead us from the death of sin to newness of life.

Either there is flood or there is drought

The parting of the Red Sea defines the exodus

A life-sustaining flow of water is seen to stream from the throne of God and of the Lamb

> Water becomes a symbol of salvation and spiritual birth

John baptizes with water for repentance, whereas Jesus is described as baptizing with the Holy Spirit and with fire (Matthew 3:11; Mark 1:8; Luke 3:16; compare John 1:33; Acts 1:5). Although Jesus did not literally baptize anyone, he instructs his disciples to baptize (Matthew 28:19). It is they who make connections with the past: Peter interprets the water of the flood as a symbol of the baptism that now saves believers (1 Peter 3:20–21), and Paul associates baptism with the crossing of the Red Sea (1 Corinthians 10:1–2).

Water, Spirit, fire... this list is beginning to sound like a table of elements (or a new rhythm-and-blues band). At an outdoor pursuits shop that I love to visit, water is one of the categories—along with others such as earth, wind, rock—for displaying related equipment for extreme conditions. There is everything from hydration systems and water filters (when you need water to drink) to special kinds of soap and towels (when you lack water for washing), to waterproof clothing and groundsheets (when you have too much water), to wetsuits and kayaks (when you want to enjoy it). All of these situations are relevant to the symbolism of water in scripture: situations of too much and too little, situations of survival, of need, of overwhelming, of pleasure.

The physical qualities point to spiritual realities. Throughout the Bible, water is a metaphor for the Spirit: its hovering (Genesis 1:2), its outpouring (Isaiah 44:3), its bringing to birth (John 3:5) and its effects in the believer (John 7:37–39; also 4:14). God is ever the spring from which both flow (Jeremiah 17:13; Revelation 22:1), but it is through Jesus that we find ultimate fulfilment of the longing expressed in Isaiah 49:10 to be led beside springs of water and never thirst again: when, as with the Samaritan woman at the well, he offers living water (John 4:10–14). What is more, he offers it freely (no costly equipment required: Revelation 21:6) to meet all needs, for our eternal survival and joy. Here is heavenly overwhelming! ■

Drinking water and
living water

David Douglas heads two non-profit water organizations, the Santa Fe-based Waterlines and Water Advocates, based in Washington DC. He is the author of 'Wilderness Sojourn' (HarperCollins, 1989), and co-author with his wife Deborah of 'Pilgrims in the Kingdom: Travels in Christian Britain' (BRF, 2004).

I write these words from Santa Fe, in the US's arid south-west, where we count ourselves fortunate to get 15 inches of rain annually. This tally compares to a nearly 30-inch average for St Andrews, Scotland, where Deborah and I once lived. Every rainfall in that beautiful university town on the Fife coast delighted us parched New Mexicans. Our enthusiasm for 'dreich' weather evoked astonishment and dismay from our Scottish neighbours.

My appreciation for rain began under grudging New Mexican skies, while experiencing occasional water shortages at our home. An unreliable

'I was thirsty
and you gave me drink'

well and pump led to a demoralizing hiss of air emerging unpredictably from empty taps. One night in 1985, our six-month-old daughter was sick. At 4am, carrying her in my arms, wearily pacing back and forth in the bedroom, I knew that our house's water supply would soon be fixed. But as I walked I found myself asking this question: 'What if you lived in a

> **Over a billion people had no access to clean drinking water**

part of the world where you never had clean water to bathe a sick child or rehydrate her?'

That question led me into years of writing magazine articles about international drinking water and sanitation. As I carried out my initial research, I had trouble comprehending the cold statistics provided by aid agencies: over a billion people had no access to clean drinking water; twice that number lacked adequate sanitation. Diseases related to water and sanitation triggered 80 per cent of sickness in the developing world and half of the world's infant mortality.

One drawback to writing is that a writer is never quite sure who is out there reading. At the end of the day, I wondered whether my words on paper should not be matched with water projects in the field, so as to get water actually flowing in a village. Before long, several friends and I started an all-volunteer charity called Waterlines, designed to link donors in the US with rural communities abroad that needed clean drinking water. In the past two decades, Waterlines has provided technical expertise and funds for over 200 drinking water projects in a dozen developing countries.

Waterlines' first projects in Mexico were funded by New Mexican churches. In the process of deciding whether their congregation should get involved in the first place, members of a church would sometimes come to an understanding of the global

© Comstock Images/Alamy

problem via their professional lens.

A scientist, for example, would speak of scarcity, noting that 97 per cent of the globe's water is saltwater, two per cent is frozen away in ice caps, and only one per cent is available for drinking, irrigation and all the other freshwater uses made by humanity. A teacher would be appalled that half of all schools in the world lack access to drinking water and sanitation. A businessman would grasp the consequences of billions of workdays lost as a result of waterborne sickness. A working mother would point out that the average African woman has to walk six kilometres each day to collect water for her family.

In addition to all these concerns, church members would recall stories of water shortage echoing through the Bible. They would know that the Hebrews were no strangers to physical thirst, particularly in the Sinai desert: 'And the Lord said to Moses, "Take the staff, and assemble the congregation, you and Aaron your brother, and tell the rock before their eyes to yield its water. So you shall bring water out of the rock for them and give drink to the congregation and their cattle"' (Numbers 20:7–8, ESV).

Then from scripture, most agonizingly, there were those two indelible words from the cross: 'After this, Jesus, knowing that all was now finished, said (to fulfil the Scripture), "I thirst"' (John 19:28). As the writer Willa Cather noted in her novel of New Mexico, *Death Comes for the Archbishop*, 'Of all our Lord's physical sufferings, only one, "I thirst", rose to His lips.'

Perhaps most importantly for any congregation debating whether or not to respond, there was the scriptural imperative of Matthew 25:35: 'I was thirsty and you gave me drink.' Jesus told his disciples that whenever they ministered to one in thirst (or hungry, sick or in prison) it was as if they were ministering to him. 'Truly, I say to you, as you did it to one of the least of these my brothers, you did it to me' (v. 40).

> 'Tell the rock before their eyes to yield its water'

Once aware of the casualty toll and scriptural mandate, many congregations chose to respond. Some supported water projects through their own ecclesiastical links abroad; other churches funded well-regarded secular water charities working in developing countries; a few advocated on behalf of increased foreign aid for international drinking water.

One Presbyterian church in Santa Fe made water part of its Lenten devotional material. The pastor preached on the worldwide need. Over a hundred members of the

Any congregation can link itself to a single project

97% of the globe's water is saltwater, 2% is frozen away in ice caps

congregation, each time they used water in their homes, set aside a contribution towards a water project at a primary school in East Africa. Paying unaccustomed attention to water usage, parishioners were stunned by how often they turned on taps. (The average American uses 100 gallons per person per day; United Kingdom per capita usage is about half that. The minimum necessary for basic health is five gallons per day—something that 1.1 billion people around the world currently lack.)

The odd nature of the world's drinking water supply—dispersed and fragmented, with hundreds of thousands of communities lacking safe, affordable access—renders the problem susceptible to small-scale, targeted responses involving one-to-one relationships. Any congregation can link itself to a single project so as to ensure an adequate water supply for a community, church, school or clinic.

Of course, the need that must be addressed also includes spiritual thirst. As Jesus told the Samaritan woman at the well: 'If you knew the gift of God, and who it is that is saying to you, "Give me a drink", you would have asked him, and he would have given you living water' (John 4:10).

The opportunity to work with villagers in obtaining clean drinking water 'tends to be so full of blessings', as one volunteer recalled, that it makes it hard to distinguish donor from recipient. Recently back from inaugurating new water cisterns at Kenyan schools, one American volunteer chronicled ceremonies marked throughout by prayer and thanksgiving:

Yesterday a village elder said he tried to think of what to give us to show how thankful he is. He said he thought about giving us a cow because he has a cow, but decided the cow would grow old and he wanted to give us something that would last. He decided asking for God's blessing on us was best.

Another volunteer reported that she had gone to inspect the capacity of water tanks, but found that it was her own Christian faith that was enlarged by the prayerful lives of Kenyans that she met.

At times, physical and spiritual thirst intersect even more tangibly. Not long ago in a village in Chiapas, Mexico, the water committee explained to a visiting architect that the remote community of thatched-roofed homes needed a better supply of drinking water. Their proposal? A cistern that could hold rainfall running off 'a large roof of tin'. The visitor listened to their proposal, and pointed out that the community 'did not have a building with a large tin roof'. 'Well, yes,' one of the villagers admitted. 'But we also need a church.'

Only briefly taken aback, the architect considered the dual need and soon provided a design—an open-air sanctuary whose tin roof channels rain via gutters into two cisterns serving double duty. One cistern is also a buttress while the other provides a church tower. The ingenious architecture offers a model for other rural sanctuaries in regions of abundant but episodic rainfall.

Here in Santa Fe, few days pass without the local newspaper chronicling a water-related story. Each year, more of the globe's newspapers come to look like Santa Fe's, as headlines report water shortages caused by dropping aquifers, pollution, deforestation and population growth. Together with climate change, water will be the environmental story of the next decade.

As consequential as global warming is likely to be, its toll on human health remains largely prospective. Water-related casualties are here today. Around the world in the next 24 hours, 4500 children will

> Together with climate change, water will be the environmental story of the next decade

die from preventable diseases caused by contaminated water and insanitary conditions. There are considerable reasons for hope, however. Between 1990 and 2004, more than 1.2 billion people gained access to improved drinking water sources, as coverage increased from 78 per cent of humanity to 83 per cent. From national governments and the UN to smaller-scale efforts of charities and private citizens, initiatives are being launched daily to improve drinking water supplies.

I spoke not long ago to someone who wanted to solve the water crisis. 'I don't want to do a single project,' he said. 'I want to solve the global problem.' So does everyone—but the problem is not capable of a single solution. Unlike a vaccine discovery for polio, solutions to the water problem are myriad.

Facing so many options, it is critical for people of faith, as they decide how to respond, to begin with prayer. By forgetting to ask what God would have them do, the risk exists, metaphorically and literally, of hewing out 'cisterns for themselves, broken cisterns that can hold no water', as the prophet Jeremiah once warned (Jeremiah 2:13).

Anchoring water work in prayer will remind congregations that they are involved not in abstract social issues but in seeking to respond to Christ. As Jesus promised, 'If anyone thirsts, let him come to me and drink. Whoever believes in me, as the Scripture has said, "Out of his heart will flow rivers of living water"' (John 7:37–38).

No congregation can conclude that the global water problem is too vast. There is a role for each member of the body of Christ to offer to others both drinking water and living water. ∎

> ...it is critical for people of faith to begin with prayer

Solutions to the water problem are myriad

Orders for an anchoress

*First go to water, any water:
brook, river, lake or sea, all speak
incessantly in tongues of liquid eloquence*

*Sit blind on bank or shore
face tipped to the wind, the sun
basting you like a baked stone*

*Hear the great swell wash and pull
the small stream chuckle and chatter*

*Rock till you too are wave
flesh flowing into the tide's sway*

*Run, run with the eddy's course
drench loose in the breaker's flail and shout*

*and then
swing still*

*and when your soul's swirl
balances
go*

the living water's pulse in your blood

VERONICA ZUNDEL

Water God's gift

Joyce Huggett is trained in counselling and spiritual direction—skills used when she and her husband David became missionaries with Interserve. These skills also led to many of her books on marriage, listening to others and listening to God. Now living in England, Joyce leads retreats and Quiet Days for missionaries and others, and spends time with her five grandchildren.

> In many countries **drinkable tap water does not exist**

'What a relief to be able to drink *tap water* without boiling it!' That's a comment I made as, after a long walk in the Derbyshire hills, I sipped and savoured a glass of iced tap water.

My husband and I had recently returned to our home in Derbyshire after spending years overseas, where our role, responsibility and privilege had been to provide pastoral care and spiritual resources for missionaries. Sometimes the missionaries would come to us in the place in Cyprus where we led retreats. Often, we would visit them in the country to which God had called them. In many of these countries, drinkable tap water does not exist, and you drink at your peril water that has not been boiled.

For countless people, drinking water is a luxury—like the children I encountered in one country we visited. Hundreds of them are homeless. They live on the bank of a river that runs through the centre of a town. In the absence of drinking water, in the stifling heat of the day, they frequently resort to drinking the filthy river water. Their hungry faces still rise before my eyes whenever I see water being wasted.

Our stay in that country was so short that we had no opportunity to minister to children like these. The reason we were there was to give water to other thirsty people—the missionaries working in that land. Like many missionaries in many countries, they were spiritually thirsty. While we were with them, ours was the joy of underlining the invitation God gives us through Isaiah: 'Come, everyone who is thirsty—here is water! ... Plenty of water, like a spring... that never runs dry' (Isaiah 55:1; 58:11, GNB).

God gives us a similar invitation in the book of Revelation when he promises a drink from the fountain filled with the water of life to anyone who is thirsty: 'Come, whoever is thirsty; accept the water of life as a gift, whoever wants it' (Revelation 22:17).

Receiving the gift

How do we receive God's promise and drink 'the water of life'? I am often asked this question. One way is to drink with our eyes. I loved doing this as I sat at my desk in our home in Cyprus. Whenever I could, I would go there to watch the rising sun slide out of the bright blue sea before soaring slowly, like a golden ball, into the cloudless blue sky. The serenity of this silent but spectacular scene raised for me a question: 'What kind of being must he be who created sunrises and sunsets as well as the azure blue sea and sky?'

> **Their hungry faces still rise before my eyes** whenever I see water being wasted

Plenty of water, like a spring... that never runs dry

I had never lived so close to the sea before but such was the magnetism of this vast expanse of water that, most days, I would walk to the nearby beach to pray. My husband and I also went there regularly to swim. As I walked and gawked and swam, I was so overwhelmed by the beauty, majesty and buoyancy of the sea that often I would find myself caught up in the kind of experience that the great woman of prayer Catherine of Siena described so beautifully: 'You, O eternal Trinity, are a deep sea into which the more I enter, the more I find, and the more I find, the more I seek. O sea profound, what more could you give me than yourself?'

Over the years I have feasted on those words as well as feasting on the sight of the sun-splashed sea. I also echo those words and, as I pray, I marvel that the deep sea of the holy Trinity—Father, Son and Holy Spirit—not only welcomes me but supports and refreshes my spirit in the same way that the Mediterranean Sea used to buoy up my body when I had the joy of swimming in it.

> **Overwhelmed by the beauty, majesty and buoyancy of the sea**

Responding to the gift

My husband and I now live in England, in an apartment that provides us with glimpses of the sea. Our home is also close to the beach, which means that it is easy to go there early in the morning where the vast expanse of water, the splendour of the sunrise and the sight and sound of seagulls squabbling over the shellfish being washed on to the shore fill me with awe and wonder and childlike delight. With equal delight, I watch how the waves wash away the flotsam and jetsam and litter that lie in the sand, as well as the way, little by little, the sea water seems to be reshaping the beach.

'Change *me*' is the prayer I often pray as I watch the water's many ministries. 'Cleanse *me*. May I bring food to others and may my life reveal your footprints.'

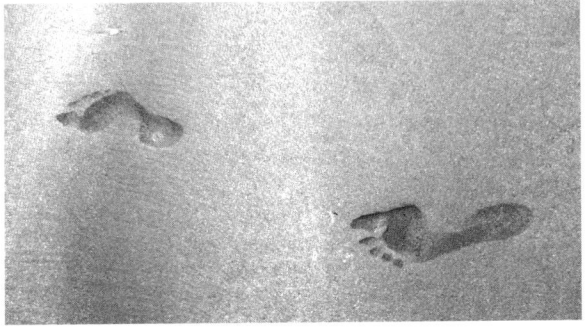

> Little by little, the sea water seems to be reshaping the beach

Every time I go to the beach or simply stand and stare at the sea from the cliff top, I marvel as I contemplate this cameo of God's creativity—so much so that I echo many songs sung by the psalmists, particularly this one:

The Lord is the great God,
the great King above all gods…
The sea is his, for he made it,
and his hands formed the dry land.
Come, let us bow down in worship,
let us kneel before the Lord our Maker.
PSALM 95:3, 5–6 (TNIV)

I marvel as I contemplate this cameo of God's creativity

Milford Sound, New Zealand

my spirit soars silently

The fiord is rather like your life

Often, I find, the glory and the grandeur before me is so great that I am stopped in my tracks. My body can do nothing but stand still, my eyes can do nothing but stare while my spirit soars silently and can do nothing but give God heartfelt praise and gratitude for symbols of his grandeur. The day before I wrote this article, for example, the strong beams of the afternoon summer sun shone so serenely on the sea, which had seemingly turned to gold, that I found myself silenced and stilled, able to whisper over and over again just one word: 'Glory!' Then came a short prayer: 'You are the King of Glory.'

Being changed by the gift

In many countries of the world, as we have seen, people have little or no access to drinking water. In many other countries, people can be changed

> **The deep sea of the holy Trinity not only welcomes me but supports and refreshes my spirit**

simply by contemplating the Creator as they marvel at the wonder of water or tune in to the message God gives through this powerful visual aid.

I think of the time when my husband and I visited Milford Sound in New Zealand. While he was queuing to buy tickets for the boat that would enable us to explore the fiord at leisure, I was marvelling so much at the beauty that I determined to discover more about the magnificent expanse of water before me. My research revealed that the top 40 metres of the water consisted of melted snow. These metres provide a home for creatures that thrive in fresh water. Underneath this top layer of water, though, lies a hidden mass of salt water that never sees the sunshine but provides a home for certain unique sea creatures.

As I marvelled at this mystery, a small voice that I took to be God's voice whispered to me: 'The fiord is rather like your life. You also have an upper layer where you know my Spirit is at work. But there is another deep, hidden layer that also needs to be owned and explored. These are also parts of your God-given personality that must be both named and befriended.'

I turned those words over and over in my mind and heart as we boarded the boat and absorbed the beauty that surrounded us on all sides: the stillness of the sky, the wonder of the water, the splendour of the snowcapped mountains. That day, and whenever I look at pictures of Milford Sound, I find myself echoing another observation made by the psalmist: 'The voice of the Lord is over the waters… The voice of the Lord is powerful' (Psalm 29:3–4, TNIV). ∎

Give God heartfelt praise and gratitude for these symbols of his grandeur

O sea profound, what more could you give me than yourself?

Reflections from a Christian Surfer

Michael Volland is a member of Christian Surfers UK. He was recently ordained as a Pioneer Minister in the Church of England, commissioned by the Bishop of Gloucester to plant a 'fresh expression' of church among 18–35s in the city centre.

I love to surf. I don't do it so much now that I have two small children, but it's still in my blood and when I'm near the sea I long to paddle out into the swell and ride the waves. There is something amazing about being in the cold, heaving mass of the ocean. As a surfer, you sit far enough from the shore to be faced only with the horizon, the hum of the wind and the feeling of legs dangling in chilly water. When I sit on my board a hundred metres out, I often have a deep realization that God is there. I find myself feeling more alive than ever as I look out to sea, waiting for the next set of waves to roll in. It's a good time to thank my Creator for putting me into what he has made to enjoy it with him.

Being in the ocean gives me a sense of how tiny I am. The sheer volume of water, stretching out of sight all around me, completely uncontrollable and able to swamp me in a second, presses into me a deep respect for nature and for my God. It also brings home to me the fact that life is an infinitely precious gift, that my times are in God's hands and that, whether I feel it or not, I am completely dependent on him at every moment.

Once, I paddled out alone off the coast of Northumbria. There was a heavy mist hanging over the sea and, as I sat with the water lapping over my legs, a regular, uncanny sound began to come towards me over the surface. A moment later, flying at ten feet above the water, three swans in tight triangular formation emerged from the mist, flew over my head and were suddenly swallowed up by the thick, white blanket. It was a bizarre moment and one in which I felt, having left the safety of land behind, I had been allowed to see something secret, like the sights granted to explorers in unknown places.

Surfing is for me, and many other surfers, essentially a sport enjoyed alone. I love the sense of peace and the chance to think, reflect and just to 'be' that surfing allows. Having said this, surfing does generate a natural sense of community, the bond that any group of people feel when they have a particular shared experience. Surfers acknowledge each other in the water and on the beach. They engage in serious discussions over wave and weather conditions and hold animated planning sessions for adventurous surf trips. In particular, there is a special bond among surfers who are Christians. Being able to

> Having left the safety of land behind, **I had been allowed to see something secret**

Being in the ocean gives me a sense of how tiny I am

thank God for the waves and for health and strength to enjoy them is a unique privilege. Doing this with others, and calling those who don't know God to join in, is amazing.

I was in Newquay a few years ago with a whole bunch of surfers who also happened to be Christians. One evening we paddled out into a three-foot swell to pray together. We went beyond the line-up of surfers, manoeuvred into a large circle and held hands while sitting on our boards. With the sun setting over the horizon and the swell rolling beneath us towards the shore, we raised our voices to God and thanked him for his amazing creation. We also prayed for the surfers around us, in need of a relationship with the one who made

> This sensory overload contrasts beautifully with the peaceful wait for the next wave

There is a special bond among surfers who are Christians

them. Joining with my fellow Christian surfers in public, surfboard-mounted prayer had a huge effect on me—and probably on everyone who saw us. It was a profound moment of Christian community in which Jesus was truly present.

Surfing is one of the UK's fastest-growing sports. I guess this is partly due to clever marketing but, more than that, I think surfing capitalizes on the way the ocean makes us feel. We are all drawn to the ocean because it sings of space, peace, possibilities and adventure. At the very least, when we visit the shore, we like to splash at the edge of the water. Surfing gets you right into the heart of the ocean. It puts you where water enthusiastically meets land and it grabs you up in vivid moments of adrenalin-fuelled freedom.

Catching a powerful wave doesn't just engage all your senses—it forces them to extremes. Every muscle in your body is working overtime, the taste and smell of salty water cram your head, the roar of the wind mixing with the rush of the water bombards your ears, and the sight of a dark, heavy wave rising up like a wall beside you as you tear down its face is enough to make you… Well, let's just say your eyes are as wide open as they'll ever be. This sensory overload contrasts beautifully with the peaceful wait for the next wave. Surfing combines adventure and risk with contemplation and listening to the sounds of creation. In our comfortable (Western) lives, it offers a powerful way of realizing that we really are alive.

This is the attraction of surfing. Just like anything else, though, if God is not at the centre it is ultimately a meaningless activity—hence the work of Christian Surfers. These guys seek to serve the surfing community, to tap into an awareness of spirituality that many surfers have and to introduce knowledge of Jesus Christ into the midst of it.

I first went surfing in 1994, while I was at university in Newcastle (and yes, you can surf in the North Sea). Shortly after becoming reasonably confident, I came across an ad in a surfing magazine for Christian Surfers UK (CSUK). I was planning a lone surf/camping trip to north Devon to hone my newly learnt skills and wanted a place to stay and the chance of some company. I phoned what I thought would be a large organization with a swish office housed in a building with its own grounds. I got through to a relaxed guy called Mike, who put me straight. There was no office other than Mike's living room and no building or grounds. There was simply a shared love for Jesus, a passion for surfing and a desire to share that combination with other surfers and serve the surfing community in the name of Jesus. It was the vision of Mike and a few others to join in with the larger work of Christian Surfers International (originally founded in Australia) and do some work for Jesus in north Devon.

On the phone, Mike told me that I would be welcome to come down and hang out with them in Croyde, but they didn't really have anywhere I could stay other than some farm land owned by a friend near Woolacombe. I set off with my board and tent and a hunger for adventure. After a long journey and many changes of transport, an old bus dropped me in a deserted street in Croyde. I hunted around for a while until eventually I was able to knock on Mike's door and shake his hand. During the following two weeks, I met and surfed with some of the founding members of Christian Surfers UK before the organization had been properly born. It was a privilege indeed, because CSUK has since grown into a dynamic national body of Christians, highly respected by the wider surfing community and effective all over the UK at reaching those in the surf culture for Jesus.

The members of Christian Surfers UK belong to a variety of church denominations, and their mission activities take place with the knowledge and support of local churches. I'm certain that churches can learn from the approach of CSUK. These guys know that in order to reach people with the message of Jesus, it is necessary to go to where

The ocean sings of space, peace, possibilities **and adventure**

they are rather than expecting them to come to us. The Christian Surfers know the importance of passion, of having fun, of modelling life in all its fullness, of being committed to community and of being focused entirely on God, on worship and on prayer. The wider church knows that it needs to be and do these things but it's always good to be reminded from time to time by seeing it in action! ∎

The Community of Aidan and Hilda and the Holy Island of Lindisfarne

Ray Simpson is the International Guardian of The Community of Aidan and Hilda.

The Holy Island of Lindisfarne is known as the cradle of Christianity to English-speaking people. St Aidan was an Irish monk in the monastic community founded by St Columba on the isle of Iona. In 635 he initiated a mission to the largely pagan people of Northumbria—the largest of the English kingdoms created by the colonizing Anglo-Saxons—at the invitation of young King Oswald.

In contrast to the approach of other missionaries, who thought the best way to spread the gospel was by making the church the most powerful institution on earth, Aidan spread it in two ways: by memorizing, living and sharing God's word, and by modelling God's kingdom. Thus he established a missionary monastery on the strategic tidal island of Lindisfarne, within sight of the royal garrison at Bamburgh. Here, he started the first recorded school for English boys. Faith-sharing teams went out far and wide. They walked everywhere, lived simply and were loved by the ordinary people. Soon monastic churches, which were really villages of God, flourished from the Forth of Firth to the River Humber 300 miles south. They included the first and largest community for both men and women led by Hilda at Whitby.

When Aidan received money, he gave it to the poor or bought slaves their freedom. He meditated constantly on scripture, challenged the powerful when they were unjust and was both prophetic and humble. When the Irish monks went into exile from Lindisfarne after the 664 Synod of Whitby, Cuthbert became the prior. The famed Lindisfarne Gospels were produced in the scriptorium, and Alcuin, adviser to the Holy Roman Emperor, declared that Lindisfarne was the most holy place in England.

Lindisfarne was the first place in Britain to be destroyed by the Vikings. During the second millennium it became a somewhat isolated fishing community alienated from the church, but last century it evolved into an internationally known nature reserve, a centre for pilgrims and tourists. Today, about 130 people live on the island. It has some twelve fishermen, two farms, four hotels, a few cafes, shops and self-catering cottages for rent. Its two retreat houses are Marygate House and The Open Gate, the latter being an embryo mother house of the international Community of Aidan and Hilda.

The Community of Aidan and Hilda describes itself as 'a worldwide pilgrim people reconnecting us with the Spirit

> **By memorizing, living and sharing God's word, and by modelling God's kingdom**

and the scriptures, the saints and the streets, the seasons and the soil'. Members follow a Way of Life with a soul friend, based on a rhythm of prayer and study, simplicity, care for creation and mission; and they seek to weave together the separated strands of Christianity. In Britain and Ireland the Community is an Associate Body of Churches Together and has advisers from the main church streams. It believes that the 'clash of civilizations' that threatens the world is not inevitable if a 'third way' emerges in the West—a new form of Christian monasticism that convinces Muslims and others oppressed by the 'Christian West' that there is a holistic model of Christianity, which is about love, not power.

In earthing their commitment to Jesus, members draw inspiration from role models such as Aidan and Hilda, who are a sign of soul friends of different race and gender working together for the common good. People may relate to the Community in varied ways: as Friends or Explorers; as those in first, monastic, hermit or life vows; as cells, households, 'fresh expressions' of church or link churches. The Community's prayer patterns are found in the four volumes of *The Celtic Prayer Book* (published by Kevin Mayhew), which churches and networks are increasingly using.

> **The famed Lindisfarne Gospels were produced in the scriptorium**

From God's point of view, the strategic centres of the Community might emerge among the poor of Cambodia or the peace-builders of Bradford, or among the emerging churches in Africa, Australia or USA, in all of which places there are members. But it seemed right to have a small presence on Lindisfarne, once we were invited, for these reasons: multitudes who now seek an authentic spirituality with roots but without obsolescent baggage are drawn to Aidan's Isle, to reconnect with God or with a Christian community that tries to live such a spirituality today. They are looking for resources and listeners. Another reason is that the island itself, with its contemplative mode when the sea cuts it off and its hospitality mode when the tide enables access, is a symbol of the rhythm we seek to live everywhere.

What is on the island for pilgrims? For some, the island is the final stage of a pilgrimage walk, such as the 62-mile St Cuthbert's Way from Melrose to Lindisfarne. For transatlantic travellers, it can be a stop on a 'pilgrim-hop' via Ireland or Scotland. It is better, though, to chill out here for up to a week and let God reach us through the island.

St Cuthbert's Isle is accessible for three hours daily at low tide. Really keen pilgrims, who want to do what the Orthodox call a *Podvig*, stay there in prayer over a tide. Others walk the two-and-a-half miles of Pilgrim Posts

> **A holistic model of Christianity, which is about love, not power**

across the sands, linger in the Lindisfarne Gospels Garden, interact with the marvellous digital presentations of the Lindisfarne Gospels and island life at the Lindisfarne Centre, or learn how Christianity came to Northumbria at the Priory Museum, where a ticket also gives access to the ruins of the twelftth-century priory built by the Benedictines who guarded Cuthbert's Durham shrine. A modern scriptorium is housed at The Burning Light bookshop. The former URC church is now the St Cuthbert's Visitors' Centre, and its director often leads a Pilgrim Walk on Fridays in the season. St Aidan's Roman Catholic Church has a daily office, weekly mass, and 'the camp' for often needy youngsters, run by marvellous helpers from St Vincent de Paul Society.

Recently, Sister Tessa, who looks after St Aidan's, has joined the island community. St Mary's, the historic Church of England parish church, is thought to be partly on the site of St Aidan's first wooden church. Traditional Anglican Morning and Evening offices and Holy Communion are offered every day of the year. A visitor during the annual Aidan Festival Week, finding the doors open, music and activities on and off, said, 'This is menu church', which people in 'fresh expressions' often call for. The leaders of the five charitable Christian bodies with a physical presence on the island meet monthly now, and jointly offer a healing service most Wednesdays.

> **Soul friends of different race and gender working together**

> ...what is key is having 'inner space' and being **attuned to God and others**

Just a handful of Community of Aidan and Hilda members live on the island and a few others on the nearby mainland. The Open Gate has only three guest rooms. We are all volunteers and run on a shoestring. The demand is far greater than the supply—we are trying to put a quart into a pint pot—so we are engaged in a listening process. Ruth Wadey, our new warden, needs a co-warden, and we need volunteers who can come in the season. We need money to extend our

God meets people at a deep level in this 'thin place'

accommodation. I live in a cottage named Lindisfarne Retreat, between the Post Office and the Gospels Garden. One room has become the dispersed Community's office, and we pay for a part-time secretary. The main room is a silent Celtic Christian Studies Library for the use of pilgrims and guests, some of whom enrol for our Celtic e-studies courses.

How, then, do we respond to this ocean of need? The Open Gate foyer houses our Resources Centre and is open to day visitors, who can make themselves a cuppa without disturbing guests. Midday and 9pm Night Prayer, said daily Mondays to Fridays, is open to anyone who can squeeze in. We facilitate group retreats by putting retreatants up in nearby accommodation; we can sometimes offer individually guided retreats if these are agreed in advance. (When there are no group retreats we do not guarantee to provide evening meals.) We find that God meets people at a deep level in this 'thin place' without the need for fussy infrastructure; what is key is having 'inner space' and being attuned to God and others.

This hymn, entitled Aidan's Prayer for Lindisfarne, has found its way into the recently published *Celtic Hymn Book*:

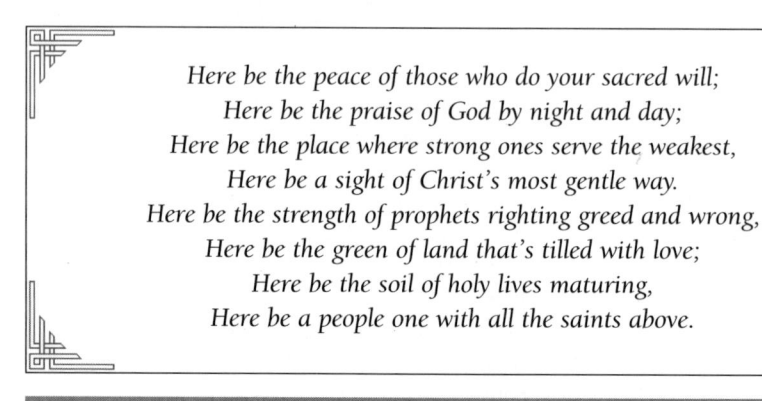

> *Here be the peace of those who do your sacred will;*
> *Here be the praise of God by night and day;*
> *Here be the place where strong ones serve the weakest,*
> *Here be a sight of Christ's most gentle way.*
> *Here be the strength of prophets righting greed and wrong,*
> *Here be the green of land that's tilled with love;*
> *Here be the soil of holy lives maturing,*
> *Here be a people one with all the saints above.*

To find out about The Community and The Open Gate, visit www.aidanandhilda.org.uk; for Lindisfarne, www.lindisfarne.org.uk. Two useful books are David Adam's *Holy Island Pilgrim Guide* and my own *A Holy Island Prayer Book* (both Canterbury Press). *A Pilgrim Way* (Kevin Mayhew) gives the story of the Community and its way of life.

Wash and flood

This is an abridged passage from 'Looking for God' by Nigel Holmes (Triangle, 1998), a book that urged its readers to search for the thumbprints of God in creation, drawing lessons from the widest wonders of the universe and from the Norfolk seashore familiar to the author, an Anglican priest with a vision for 'mission-shaped' church before the term was invented.

In John the Baptist's day, the voice of prophecy had fallen silent; then he appeared, with a message which captured the imagination of the whole community… John's baptism, a 'baptism of repentance', proclaimed it was high time to take the nation to God's laundry at the River Jordan! But the symbolism of water and the faithful preaching which accompanied it says so much more as well, if instead of letting our eyes wander over the mere surface of the river, we gaze into its depths.

We can see death in the water, two great 'drownings', Noah's flood and Pharaoh's doom, first, when a wicked world was swept away under God's righteous judgement; and second,

> **We can see death in the water, two great 'drownings'**

when Israel finally broke free from bondage to the Egyptian tyrant. We can see renewal, too, in Noah's dove with the olive branch, a new beginning, and a world ready to be born again. For Israel, we can see a nation finally emerging from forty years of pilgrimage, leaving an unbelieving generation buried in the past (still hankering for Egypt); while under Joshua's leadership, we see a new nation, setting off to claim the promised land.

We can see the healing stream, the Jordan, which the Syrian general Naaman at first glance despised, when told to wash in it to have his leprosy healed. But this is no ordinary river; it is a unique and noble torrent! It rises pristine from the living rock at Caesarea Philippi, fed by the snows of 10,000-foot-high Mount Hermon, plunging down to sea level, and then on 600 feet lower, to the Sea of Galilee, surrounded by its little towns and rugged hills. It goes on falling, along the line of the Great Rift Valley (which itself stretches 3000 miles here from Africa), on and down to Jericho, and finally to that 'world sump', the

> **Let the font be the window of our imagination**

Dead Sea, 1200 feet below sea level. There it disappears, vaporizing in the heat, leaving great mineral deposits which cover the ancient cities of Sodom and Gomorrah…

John, however, did not dwell on the past glories of the river. He spelt out the meaning of repentance for the perplexed citizens, vigilant men-at-arms and busy tax collectors of his day, as 'with many other words' he 'exhorted the people and preached the good news to them' (Luke 3:18). He blended forceful urgency with a striking humility; and the word he is associated with, 'baptize', is an energetic and humbling one. This is seen in the way the word is spelt—a Greek word whose root is: *bapt*-; so *bapto* means 'I dip'. Adding -*iz*- intensifies it; so *baptizo* means 'I dip strongly'; 'I plunge, I fill, I flood—even I drown…'.

…What can we learn from John? We must want to do what he did… We must make it our ambition to catch the attention of the whole community, fire its imagination and provoke its thirst for the living waters of spiritual reality…

What happens when we go to church? No doubt if you are a newcomer, it all seems strange these days. If you are an old hand, you simply settle down in your familiar groove. In either case, we are blind to what is really there! But God is here too, at the centre of everything, bringing the building wonderfully to life, if only we had the imaginative power to recognize his presence… Perhaps it is one of those Sundays when the church is full of flowers—forget them! They must not distract us at this stage from the water. A great rushing torrent, which continually fills the entry to the nave of every church! Why have we lost sight of something so demanding in its symbolism? …

To bring the world to life we must focus on the font. Let the font be the window of our imagination. Font means fountain, and it represents the River Jordan. Now at last we can see it, a river flooding through the nave, threatening, inviting, liberating, inspiring! Each time we enter church,

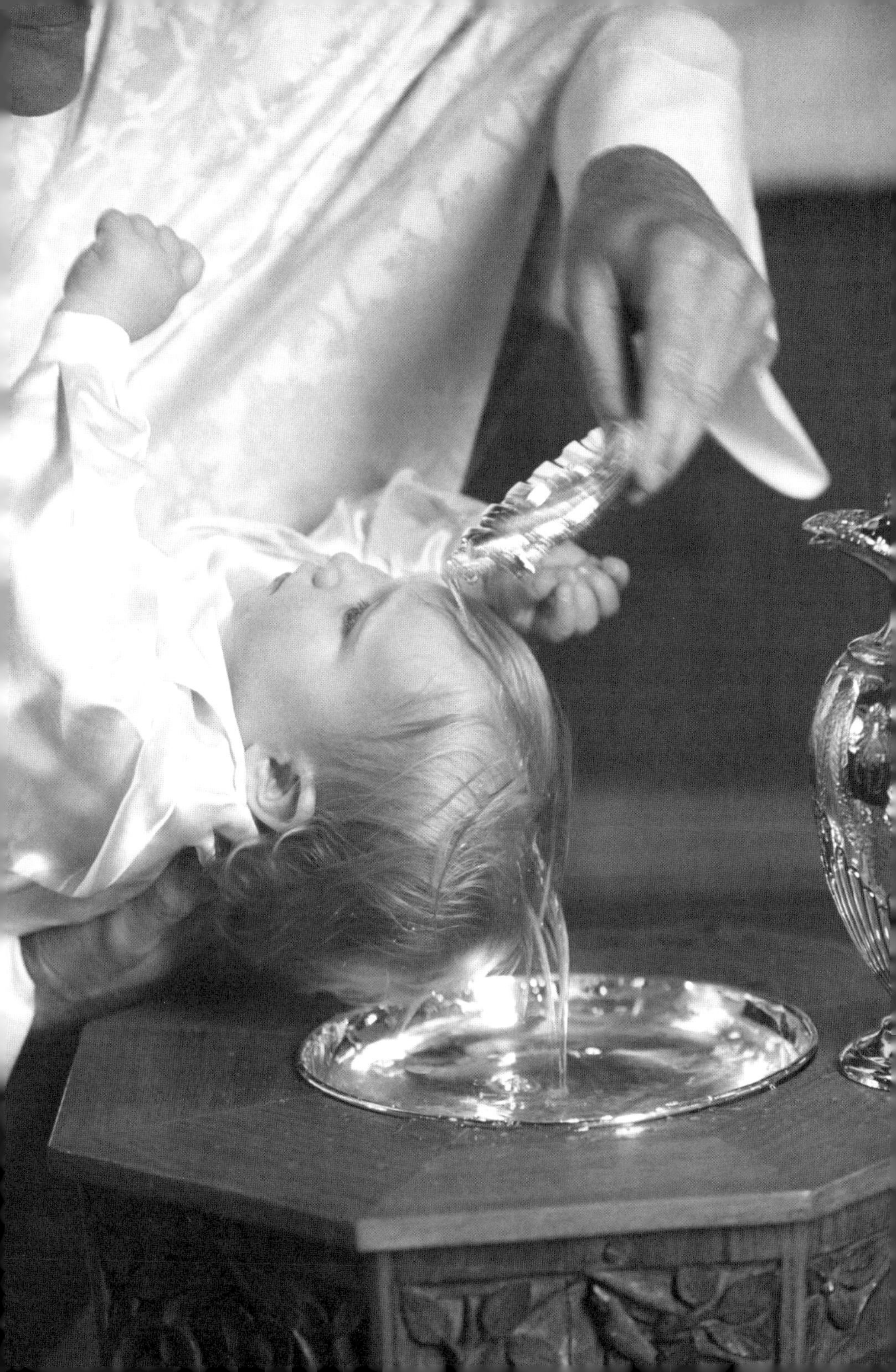

our hearts and minds should be lit up by the memory that we once crossed this river, and now live in the promised land, where heaven comes to Earth.

The church stretches itself out west to east, between this fountain and a feast. At this end, though baptism is a once-and-for-all event, we must always be ready to 'launch out into the deep' again, into the fullness of all God has for us. His grace and power are here to turn life upside down and inside out… Turning from here to the far end of the church, we set off to the feast, God's Word comes to life again. This is important, because it is his Word that ultimately washes us: 'Christ loved the Church and gave himself up for her to make her holy, cleansing her by the washing with water through the word, and to present her to himself as a radiant church, without spot or wrinkle or any other blemish, but holy and blameless' (Ephesians 5:25–27).

However, the truth of God's Word needs the power of God's Spirit; and John promised that while he baptized in water, Christ would baptize in the Holy Spirit. Like the luminescent waters of the sea, baptismal water symbolizes spiritual light and fire. Many of us start to be nervous when we see how deep God's water is. Rather than plunge into its fullness, which means letting go of what we are used to, and taking the risk of going against the stream, and perhaps ending up where we had never planned to be, we keep one foot firmly on the solid world we have grown up in, and cling to the handrail of convention. While we are rightly cautious about many things in life, we should not be so about our heavenly Father's love. Baptism commands us not merely to dip our toes in the river of God's life, but take our foot off the bottom, let go of the handrail, and learn how to swim in the full current of God's purpose for our lives… ∎

> Learn how to swim in the full current of **God's purpose**

Many of us start to be nervous **when we see how deep** God's water is

God's banquet, so simple to look at, but in Christ rich, satisfying and unfailing—the more we share of it, the more its riches grow.

Once we have learnt how to recognize the pictures that can be switched on in a church, so much of

Ministering angels

This is an extract from Carol Hathorne's book 'Assist our Song' (BRF, 2006), which looks at what the Bible has to say about angels and shares stories of 'angelic encounters'.

God our Father uses ordinary human beings in the role of ministering angels, sometimes in the most unexpected ways and places.

'I'm a retired teacher,' explains Sarah. 'Some years ago, when I had just been through a painful divorce, I was feeling in real spiritual darkness. One afternoon, after all the children had left the classroom, I sat at my school desk and just wept.

'Suddenly I felt someone touch my arm. I turned, and there was a boy from my class standing there. He had dark curls and blue eyes. He was a quiet boy who really looked a bit like an angel. He looked up at me, then, silently, he went to the corner where the sink was. He took a cup and filled it with water.

'"Here, Mrs Masters," he said. "Drink this!"

'I took the water and drank it, and in that moment, crazy though it might sound, I knew that everything had changed. God was close to me, and I could cope with whatever was going to happen in the future.'

That young boy had felt compelled to stay behind to help his teacher in a small but nevertheless vital way—the way of love, which, by its very simplicity, reminds us of Jesus' commandment to love one another as he has loved us. Jesus himself performed the most lowly of loving acts when he washed his disciples' feet at the last supper. He became a servant as he cared for their most basic needs.

Read John 13:12–15.

Music for the soul:
Many waters cannot quench Love

Gordon Giles is vicar of St Mary Magdalene's Church, Enfield, north London. He contributes to BRF's 'New Daylight' notes and has also written 'The Music of Praise' (2002), 'The Harmony of Heaven' (2003) and 'O Come, Emmanuel' (2005) for BRF.

Many waters cannot quench Love, neither can the floods drown it. Love is strong as death. Greater love hath no man than this, that a man lay down his life for his friends.

Who his own self bare our sins in his own body on the tree, that we, being dead to sin should live unto righteousness.

Ye are washed, ye are sanctified, ye are justified, in the name of the Lord Jesus; ye are a chosen generation, a royal priesthood, a holy nation, that ye should shew forth the praises of him who hath called you out of darkness into his marvellous light.

I beseech you, brethren, by the mercies of God, that ye present your bodies, a living sacrifice, holy, acceptable to God, which is your reasonable service.

WORDS: SONG OF SONGS 8:6–7; JOHN 15:13; 1 PETER 2:9, 24; 1 CORINTHIANS 6:11; ROMANS 12:1
MUSIC: JOHN IRELAND (1879–1962)

Many will know of John Ireland's hymn tune 'Love Unknown', written in 1919 specially for the hymn 'My Song is Love Unknown'. Pianists may know his charming miniature called *The Holy Boy*, or even his piano concerto, while choral singers may well know this beautiful anthem, which is usually entitled *Greater Love hath no man*.

Born on 13 August 1879 in Bowden, near Manchester, John Nicholson Ireland's family moved to London when he was 14, and he spent most of his life there, with a brief period in the Channel Islands (he just escaped from the German invasion of Guernsey in June 1940). At 16 he was the youngest person to gain the FRCO (Fellowship of the Royal College of Organists), and in 1904 he became organist at St Luke's Church, Chelsea, where he remained for 22 years. He was also Professor of Musical Composition at the Royal College of Music and a senior examiner for the Associated Board. In 1953 he retired to West Sussex, where he died in 1962, aged 82.

Ireland was a very self-critical man, so much so that he destroyed many of his early compositions. Yet his anthem of 1912, *Greater Love*, has survived and is frequently sung today by church and cathedral choirs. It was written for Charles Macpherson, who was then Assistant Director of Music at St Paul's Cathedral. A later, orchestral version appeared in 1924.

Although the theological message of Ireland's anthem is quite complex, it is a masterly juxtaposition of texts. This is not just poetry, however, but music, and in the music another dimension is added, illustrating and underlining the deeper meanings of scripture. Ireland begins the piece

> **Human love that is divinely inspired is so strong that it does not wash off**

The power of the sea is one of the greatest forces known on earth

with a brief introduction before the choir gently sing the opening phrase, from the Song of Songs. Human love that is divinely inspired is so strong that it does not wash off: there is no detergent or power of water that will erase it—it is permanent as a tattoo. Here we encounter the force and power of water, not just the strength of love. They are matched, and love wins, but only just.

The power of the sea is one of the greatest forces known on earth (which is why it is so significant that Jesus quells the storm in Mark 4:35–40). So, as the fire of love is described as 'strong as death', unquenchable by any water, the music swells like a rising tide until, held back only briefly, it crashes into the line 'Greater love hath no man' and then subsides.

As baptized Christians, we have an inheritance as a royal priesthood

> **The music builds once again, riding a crest of a wave**

Soprano and bass soloists then intone the words from 1 Peter before the choir repeat the words as the music builds once again, riding a crest of a wave to fanfares on the words of Paul, 'ye are washed', the crux of the whole work. It is in the cleansing waters of baptism that we begin our Christian journey. As baptized Christians, we have an inheritance as a royal priesthood, which takes us back to the moment that marked the beginning of Jesus' ministry when he submitted himself to the baptism of John (Mark 1:9–11). It is membership of the Christian family that confers both the duty and the ability to love with a love as strong as death—to lay down one's life if necessary, for that is what our Lord did for us. The great German theologian Dietrich Bonhoeffer, who himself suffered a martyr's death, wrote in *The Cost of Discipleship* that 'Christ calls each one of us to come and die'. Such a duty is not fashionable these days, even among committed Christians, but in some parts of the world it is still a very real prospect. We are called to love with a strong love because Christ has shown us just how powerful love can be (it is stronger than any force of water, even than death itself).

The points of musical emphasis punctuate the text, breaking Love's message like waves on the shore. The fanfares also reflect the royalty of the priesthood before a new theme emerges, an expansive, ever-so-English tune building up to the phrase 'into his marvellous light'. Then the tide subsides on a noticeable key change, ushering in a calm after the storm, in which we are entreated to present ourselves as holy before God. Becalmed in beauty, the music slows down to the end, fading away into air that has been refreshed by the vigours of a deluge now past. ■

Music to listen to

Greater Love hath no man by John Ireland. Available on a CD called *Remembrance*, released by Hyperion (ref: CDA67398) in 2003. Sung by St Paul's Cathedral Choir, directed by John Scott.

Readings for reflection

Mark 4:35–40

The hidden life of the oyster

Emma Garrow is a freelance writer who has worked with 'The Church of England Newspaper' and Fresh Expressions. She lives in Bath and worships at Bath Abbey.

We all have an idea of what a pearl looks like. It is small, white and perfectly round. It is worn by film stars and ladies in twinsets, or brides on their wedding day. It hangs from the ear of a model in a precious and world-famous painting. A string of pearls is an ultimate gift, as worthy of a meaningful occasion as a chain of gold.

Yet pearls, so uniform in the popular mind, come in a rich variety of form and colour. Chinese freshwater pearls, for example, are oval. Button pearls are flat on one side and round on the other. Those known as Biwa pearls are elongated. Pearls may be white or they may be black, with tones of pink and green in the range, depending on the originating mollusc and water conditions during growth. Deeper tones are found in the mother-of-pearl shell lining inside the molluscs, which is also prized.

The best-known originator of a pearl is, of course, the oyster, but there is more than just one type of oyster, which in itself is just one in the family of shell creatures that may produce a pearl.

Wild pearls, like many wild things, are as hard to find nowadays as a four-leaf clover. Whereas, in times gone by, the beautiful wild pearl discovered by chance formed the stuff of romance, today irritants are inserted into molluscs by technicians to supply the world market with the real thing, while artificial pearls are produced as a supplement. The

> Wild pearls, like many wild things, are as hard to find nowadays as a four-leaf clover

irritant will be more than just a grain of sand swallowed by the oyster in the water, as it is quite capable of ridding itself of such minuscule aliens. Something larger must do the job, such as a piece of shell or coral or a parasite. The oyster protects itself from this irritant by coating it in layers of the same substance, known as nacre, with which it produced its own shell. Nacre builds up in layers, forming the pearl we find when the oyster is opened.

What comes into being as the result of an irritation is a desirable object, reflecting light from the depths of its being as the crystals in the nacre respond to the sun. Within its hard and knobbly shell, the soft creature of the oyster has made of an uncomfortable, unwanted, invading ingredient something substantial and of value.

Of course, not all oysters are cultivated for pearl production. Some are cultivated to eat. Here the oyster's reputation is again as something of worth, something that has a meaning beyond its simple purpose. It is both a health-giving and a legendary foodstuff. These two qualities are linked together, oysters being high in zinc, which is particularly necessary for male sexual health. Casanova was said to eat a great quantity for breakfast each day. They are also a source of Omega 3, which lowers cholesterol levels and provides other vitamins and minerals which, among other things, promote an active brain.

Since molluscs have been around for hundreds of millions of years, their fruits have been a part of humanity's inheritance since human life began. Throughout history, pearls were the preserve of the wealthy. Cleopatra fed powdered pearl to Mark Antony in wine; Queen Elizabeth I adored them. But even great figures of the past rarely possessed a perfect pearl. In fact, one sign that a pearl is genuine and not artificial is its gritty texture. As the oyster produces its layers of nacre, it does not make a full coating each time, causing what are referred to as 'imperfections' in the pearl. These do not reduce the value; rather, they prove the worth. Any pearl, extremely rare, that matches the mythic description of 'perfect' is considered to be of gem quality, but since these account for but a tiny percentage of the millions of pearls harvested each year, the slight imperfections are accepted as a mark of authenticity.

In the Bible, where pearls are mentioned it is their high value that makes them worthy of reference. The twelve gates of the holy city in Revelation are each made of a single pearl. Pearls form part of the beauty that we are to expect in the heavenly realm. This is not surprising when we remember that Jesus told the parable of a merchant who sought fine pearls. Finding 'one of great value, he went away and sold everything he had and bought it' (Matthew 13:45, NIV).

From the oyster, a creature older than humanity, has come and still comes a precious object—the stuff of legend, a symbol of beauty and perfection—and this as a result of struggle. Even through the tight cracks of the oyster shell, so craggy and prohibitive, alien elements find their way inside. As the oyster works to protect itself from the invader, it creates a thing of beauty. In this it reflects the struggle of creation itself, described by the apostle Paul:

I consider that our present sufferings are not worth comparing with the glory that will be revealed in us. The creation waits in eager expectation for the sons of God to be revealed. For the creation was subjected to frustration, not by its own choice, but by the will of the one who subjected it, in hope that the creation itself will be liberated from its bondage to decay and brought into the glorious freedom of the children of God.
ROMANS 8:18–21 (NIV)

> **One sign that a pearl is genuine and not artificial is its gritty texture**

As we struggle to smooth the irritants that enter beneath our outer protective barriers, those thorns and hard-cornered stones of encounter or experience, which lodge in our inner being, we share in the wider story of the struggle of creation towards glory. Finding the God-given nacre within our own being, we can create something worthy of offering in the heavenly realm, all the more precious for the marks of imperfection that show it to have been born out of genuine struggle and not fabricated for success.

In the simple tale of the oyster, and in the lustre of the pearl, is glimpsed a reflection of the story of our redemption. ■

At the well of *healing*

> Come, all you who are thirsty, come to the waters; and you who have no money, come, buy and eat… and your soul will delight in the richest of fare.
>
> ISAIAH 55:1A, 2B (NIV)

Anne Hibbert is an ordained minister in the Church of England, who lives in Royal Leamington Spa. She is the founder and Director of 'The Well' Christian Healing Centre.

God very quickly drew a team around me

For many years Royal Leamington Spa was a renowned spa town, boasting medicinal waters that would cure many diseases and sicknesses. At the height of its popularity, the town had 81 hotels and seven open wells that resourced the many baths. Much of its present-day prosperity originated from this period.

Not knowing this at the time, it was a huge surprise when I felt God speak to me in June 2002, giving me a vision to open a Christian healing centre called *The Well*. I was sitting in a friend's garden, enjoying the sunshine, when I believe I heard God say, 'Anne, I am about to open up the ancient wells of healing here in Leamington Spa and just as people came from far and wide in the past so they will return. You will see me work in power and this time their healing will last.' And right at the end God said, 'It will be called *The Well*.'

After much heart-searching, fasting and consultation with local clergy,

Anne Hibbert at the sign of The Well:
'We long to see people discover the healing and liberating truth about Jesus...'

I went to see my bishop, Colin of Coventry. He listened to my story and said, 'Anne, I have no money to give to you but you have my blessing. Go and open *The Well*!'

God very quickly drew a team around me who helped me continue to consult with local clergy. He called a friend of mine, Tim Hollingdale, at around the same time as me. We wrote a healing training course, using material from the John Wimber five-step model of healing prayer. In summer 2003, 58 Christians from 25 local churches joined our training course—a huge encouragement to us. Finally, in February 2004, we opened our doors weekly to the public in the Royal Pump Rooms in Leamington, on Tuesday afternoons and evenings and Wednesday mornings. In time, we hope to be open six days a week.

Since June 2002, I have been learning at a massive rate with God. I have had to ask some big questions, like 'Does God heal today?' But as I looked into the Bible, it became alarmingly clear that being involved in Jesus' healing ministry today was not an option but a mandate. The disciples, who were the embryonic Church, were empowered to work the same ministry that Jesus worked, and the results (recorded in Acts) are a sequence of miracles, healings, signs and wonders. There is a close link between these miraculous events and the growth of the early Church. The Church grew where the gospel was preached and signs and wonders occurred. The early Church anticipated supernatural involvement from God, and even the way it was led relied heavily on visions, prophecies and other forms of revelation. Fortunately, we have accounts of both success and failure in Acts and the epistles.

Jesus came not only to bring the kingdom of God, to save and to heal, but also to pass on to others this healing ministry, so that they might share in the growth of the kingdom. We, as the Church, were commissioned 2000 years ago to announce the good news to all creation through the healing 'signs' that would accompany and authenticate the message wherever it was preached.

So the basis for a healing ministry today is that Jesus expects his Church

> Being involved in Jesus' healing ministry today is not an option but a mandate

The early Church anticipated supernatural involvement from God

to continue the ministry he started. With Jesus, the kingdom of God came with power. Before his ascension, he commissioned his followers not only to 'go and make disciples' but also to 'teach them to obey everything I have commanded you' (Matthew 28:19–20). One of the things Jesus commanded his followers to do was to pray for healing for the sick—and that is our mandate, too.

Our vision for *The Well* is of a place where people can come from far and wide for prayer for healing. It is a safe place where the sick, hurting and wounded can come so that our team can pray over them in the name of Jesus. It is a place where anyone can come, regardless of their race or religion, wealth or health.

The following are our values at *The Well*, which affect everything we do:

- *The Well* is missionary in that it exists to fulfil the purpose and vision for which it was established under God. It operates in a way that is dependent on God for all it needs to fulfil that purpose. It is not a business (although we need to be business-like); it is not a church (although we do things that are church-like); it is not a community (although we need to relate to each other in a community-like way).

- *The Well* is Christian, with Jesus at the centre, and we seek to operate as the servants of God—Father, Son and Holy Spirit. We need to operate as part of 21st-century Leamington but in a distinctive way that marks us out as Christian.

- *The Well* is biblical, and we seek to operate within the best principles and practices set out in the Bible.

47

Christian... biblical... prayerful... caring... aims for excellence

Anyone can come, regardless of their race or religion, wealth or health

- *The Well* is prayerful, and we seek to operate with prayer at the centre of all that we do; prayer is the powerhouse of our ministry.
- *The Well* is caring, and we seek to treat our guests and team members with care, compassion and dignity.
- *The Well* aims for excellence, and as such we seek to operate to the highest possible standards, within the law, wisely using the resources at our disposal.

As part of the local church network, *The Well* is playing a unique part in restoring community in Leamington Spa and beyond. We long to see people living fuller lives because of better health. More than that, we long to see people discover the healing and liberating truth about Jesus so that they will not only have healthier bodies, but also healthier hearts, emotions, souls and lives.

We can also see that others will want to find out more about what is going on here, and that as people come to be healed themselves, so they will go home wanting to see their friends and neighbours receive what they've got. They will take with them a vision for healing in their own communities. To do that, they will need to set up their own healing centres. To help make this a reality, we have hosted a number of 'come and see' sessions for church leaders, to see us in operation and receive prayer for themselves.

Since we opened, *The Well* has received a steady and growing stream of guests through the doors for prayer. A welcome sign is placed outside on the main street and prayer teams are available to pray for anyone who walks in. Guests do not need to book in advance for appointments, but they can do so if they are particularly ill or travelling a long distance. By September 2006, 967 guests had visited us and, because some returned for further prayer, we had offered over 2500 appointments.

We have many wonderful and encouraging stories of our guests' encounters with God. A few months ago, a woman dropped in to visit us, who was not a Christian. She simply saw the sign outside and walked in off the street for prayer. During her prayer appointment she suddenly opened her eyes and said, 'Oh, this is much better than going to a spiritualist!'

Many people have written to thank The Well's prayer team for their help. Some have also included personal testimonies of healing (you can see more of these testimonies on our website: www.wellhealing.org). We hear many stories of God blessing people, giving them the strength to face their situations, giving them relief from pain and in some cases complete healing from their physical condition. Many of our guests have emotional issues related to their physical conditions and often we hear of how God is healing the person as well as the illness. Here are three testimonies, which are used with permission.

On 23 May I came to The Well *for the first time for prayer. As soon as I walked in, I felt our Lord's presence and I just knew it was right for me to be there. Two ladies prayed with me for arthritis in both my knees, which I have had for some time and have found it very hard to walk. On Tuesday night the Lord healed me and I am free of pain and can walk and go up stairs freely. Thank you, Lord. I was also healed the same night of arthritis in the middle finger of my left hand. (LH)*

I feel, today, God has called me to come out of my tomb of darkness. I feel a cloak of shame has fallen off me. I feel he wants to hold my head up. God beckoned me into The Well… *last night. I feel God has done further sexual abuse healing. I feel* The Well *is an oasis in the desert. It's a welcoming, safe place to be. There is an atmosphere of love. (Ann)*

> We have many wonderful and encouraging stories of our guests' **encounters with God**

Over a number of visits and after receiving prayer at The Well, *I'm now a free man. My life has completely changed and I now realize how valued and loved I am by God. I want to thank* The Well *for their professional approach and sensitivity around the matters concerning my issues. I always felt at ease and never had a problem with being open because what I said was always received with empathy and compassion. (DM)*

We continue to struggle with the age-old question: 'Why doesn't God heal everyone when we pray?' Healing may be a mystery, but our part at *The Well* is to pray in faith, and the rest is up to God! ■

John Newton's
life of amazing grace
(1725–1807)

Jean Watson, an ex-MK (missionary kid) brought up in China, trained as a teacher but took up writing when her three children were small, and is now a grandmother to their three children. She is currently training to be a spiritual director.

Life under a brutal slave master brought no improvement to his lot

John Newton's most famous hymn reflects something of its author's spiritual journey. Having lived an immoral life for many years, John Newton felt overwhelmingly grateful for the experience of God's mercy, washing over him like the waves of the ocean flooding a parched, polluted shore.

An only child, John was close to his mother but never developed the same bond with his father, a shipmaster who was often away from home. Elizabeth Newton brought her son up in the Christian faith, and their short time together was to bear fruit much later. Her death from TB when John was only seven was a devastating blow. On top of this, John Newton senior remarried and sent his son off to boarding school. Then, when the boy was only 11 years old, he took him off to sea. They made several voyages together over the next six years.

On a visit to Kent, the young John met the love of his life, Mary Catlett, although it was to be some years before he was able to marry her. His father wanted his son to set himself up in the shipping business overseas. John had other ideas, but they were rudely thwarted when he was seized and press-ganged into service on a man-of-war. An unsuccessful attempt to desert earned him punishment and demotion. Only the thought of Mary, he said later, kept him from trying to murder the captain or committing suicide. He got himself transferred to a vessel engaged in the African slave trade, but life under a brutal slave master brought no improvement to his lot.

By this time, he had fallen into a way of life far removed from anything inculcated by his early Christian upbringing. In fact, by the time a sea captain, sent by his father, discovered his whereabouts and offered to rescue him, he had risen to the ranks of captain on his own slave ship and had hopes of making his fortune through the trade.

Then, however, he had a terrifying experience at sea. A dreadful storm struck and, fearing for his life, John cried out to God for mercy. Although badly damaged, the ship made it to land, convincing John that God had heard and answered his prayer. He regarded this experience as his conversion, but many ups and downs in his spiritual life were to follow.

His newfound faith did not immediately cause him to quit the slave trade. It did, however, prompt him to ensure that the slaves on his ship were treated humanely, and later he came to be appalled by and to repent of his involvement with the cruel trafficking in human lives.

Meanwhile, at the age of 25, John married Mary. Theirs was to prove a happy union, although they had no children of their own. They adopted two orphaned nieces from the Catlett family, one of whom died as a child. Five years after his marriage, John had a serious illness, which forced him to

God's mercy, washing over him like the waves

give up seafaring. He then worked as a surveyor of tides in Liverpool, and it was here that he came under the influence of the famous evangelical preacher George Whitefield and, later, of the great John Wesley.

During his life at sea, Newton had tried to educate himself and now he began to study theology in earnest. He decided to try for ordination in the Anglican Church. One bishop turned him down but eventually another accepted him and he became the curate at Olney in Buckinghamshire. His dynamic personality and preaching, as well as his enthusiasm and commitment, soon got him noticed and over the next 16 years his congregation and ministry kept growing. He once wrote, 'My grand point in preaching is to break the hard heart and to heal the broken one.'

> His newfound faith did not immediately cause him to quit the slave trade

The sea tossed him back to God

It was at Olney that he became great friends with a man whose heart was often wrung, if not broken, by severe depression. Despite this, William Cowper helped John with his ministry and together they wrote many hymns. A list of Newton's enduring and best-loved hymns would have to include, along with 'Amazing grace', 'How sweet the name of Jesus sounds' and 'Glorious things of thee are spoken'.

Several of Cowper's hymns reflected something of his diffident, gentle temperament and his struggle between faith and doubt. At times he felt that he was rejected and condemned by God. Some have blamed Newton's Calvinism and robust character for exacerbating Cowper's depression, but Newton was a kinder and warmer person than such criticism implies; as witness, for example, this extract from a letter to his friend: 'I know not that I ever saw you for a single day since your calamity came upon you, in which I could not perceive as clear and satisfactory evidence that the grace of God was with you, as I could in your brighter and happier times.'

At the age of 55, Newton accepted the living at the church of St Mary Woolnoth in London. There his influence and ministry as preacher, pastor and writer continued to flourish and grow and he became friends with many well-known evangelicals, including William Wilberforce, whose anti-slavery campaign he supported.

When Mary died of cancer, John was grief-stricken and his failing health and sight added to his difficulties. His surviving daughter, Betsy, supported him lovingly until, at the age of 82, he died peacefully and was buried beside his wife.

It would be interesting to know if John ever reflected on the influence of the sea on his life. It brought him many terrible experiences and was the context for his dissolute behaviour, but it also tossed him back to God, at whose amazing grace he never ceased to marvel. ■

The seawater kingdom

Late morning, and they were down at the slipway, she and her grandfather, and spread out on the slippery stones was the skeleton of a canoe. The sun was high above the cliff behind them, shining warm on their backs.

She watched him at work. He was kneeling down, slotting long wooden poles together and fastening struts in place, before sliding the frame into the canoe skin so that it stretched tight. *How soon can we go?*

Somehow he knew what she was thinking as she stood next to him, shifting impatiently. He smiled up at her, his brown face creasing in the way she loved.

'Won't be long.'

The sunlight stretched to the horizon, and there, shadowy in the distance, she could see the islands. They were no more than stubs of rock now, with the

Naomi Starkey is the editor of 'Quiet Spaces'. She also edits 'New Daylight' Bible reading notes, as well as commissioning BRF's range of books for adults.

The sun was high above the cliff...

> Slotting long wooden poles together and fastening struts in place

I am going to find him, to tell him it is safe to return

sea still high, but if she had the binoculars she would be able to see a cluster of huts perched on top. As the water retreated, more land would appear, until the islands doubled in size—for a few hours, at least. *'A seawater kingdom with one lonely king.'* Her grandfather's words. *But what does he mean? How can a king be lonely? And live in a hut?*

'Time to go.'

With a grunt of effort, he carried the canoe to the water's edge. Her job was to hold it steady while he loaded seats, paddle, rug and picnic bag. Then he lowered her in, laced tightly in her lifejacket, and lastly sat himself down behind her. Together they pushed off.

With a few swift paddle strokes the canoe pulled away from the slipway and began moving along the protecting arm of the breakwater. The open sea beyond was reassuringly calm, with the current of the ebb tide helping to carry them out towards those remote island rocks.

Silence, except for the slap of water on the canvas sides, the dip of the paddle first on the right and then the left, the echo of seagulls from the sandy beach round the headland, where the first holidaymakers would already be spreading their towels and sun cream.

'Would you like to come with me?' He had asked her a few days ago, describing the seawater kingdom that grew and diminished with the tides. 'Does anybody live there?' She pictured having the place to themselves, a chance to play one of her hours-long made-up games.

The answer was not what she expected: 'Just one man. I want to pay him a visit.' She wanted to know more. Did he live on the islands all the time? That was when her grandfather told her that this man was like a lonely king. 'Alone in a seawater kingdom. But I am going to ask him to come home. He doesn't need to be afraid any more.' She did not understand that. 'How could anybody be afraid of coming home?'

The reply came slowly: 'Long ago, people accused him of doing something very wrong. He was afraid, so he ran away, and he has stayed alone on the islands ever since. And now I am going to find him, to tell him it is safe to return.'

She looked at her grandfather, paddling with long, steady strokes, eyes gazing past her at the blue-green sea. She wondered how he knew about this lonely man, why it was his job to go and find him. Sometimes, though, when she asked question after question, he would fall silent and simply smile at her. 'You don't need to know it all now.' That was what he would sometimes say to her.

What she did know was that he seemed to have a habit of finding lost and lonely people; she'd lost count of the times when, as they walked somewhere together, they would cross a street, take an unexpected turn, walk down a different road—and find somebody in their path, as if he had known they would be there, waiting for the comfort and consolation that he always brought. He seemed to know exactly what they needed before they spoke or sobbed out their story.

Now the slipway and even the breakwater had dwindled, merging into the succession of bays that curved around the coast. The canoe glided forward over water that was glassy smooth and clear, with a slow swell that never broke the surface but swirled the seaweed forests deep below.

Already the islands were much nearer and she could count four now, with smaller outcrops appearing as the tide continued to recede. Three huts on the largest island, two on the next in size; one by itself, on the smallest island, with a tiny patch of sand in front of it. *Who lives in the other ones?*

He seemed to have a habit of finding **lost and lonely people**

> As the water retreated, more land would appear

> Only a narrow channel of water separated one island from the other

'Holiday homes.' Her grandfather answered her thoughts again, speaking aloud for the first time since they set out. 'He likes to keep an eye on them for the owners. They don't come here much.'

In another few minutes, they had to watch for a safe channel as they drew closer. Her grandfather paddled cautiously, watching out for a white paint marker that, lined up with another unpainted rock, steered them into a tiny man-made harbour on the largest island. As they drifted over the last stretch of water, a figure appeared from behind one of the huts—a man with a blue woollen hat pulled low on his forehead and a rusty bucket in one hand. His white-flecked beard reached his chest. *A bit like Father Christmas.* But he was not smiling.

She sensed her grandfather sitting very still behind her. 'There he is.' She heard him take a deep breath before calling out, 'Please—may we come ashore? I'd like to talk to you.'

The man stared at them and then nodded, once. Jerking his head to indicate that they should follow, he began walking away towards the solitary hut. The sea was now so low that only a narrow channel of water separated one island from the other, and he stepped over it easily, making his way over the waste of rocks without stumbling or slipping. Then he turned again to watch the approach of the visitors.

She clambered from the canoe on to the low concrete step that formed the harbour wall, one foot splashing clumsily in a pool. The wind felt cold out here and she began to shiver.

'Here.' She felt the picnic rug spread round her shoulders, and then her grandfather pulled the canoe higher out of the retreating water, securing it by a rope round one of the rocks marking the harbour.

'This is what I want you to do for me.' She nodded as he went on: 'Stay here, near the canoe.

You know not to go in the sea or climb on the big boulders. Don't come looking for me until I call you. And don't worry if it takes a bit of time.' And he left her, striding over the stones and seaweed, across to where the lonely king stood waiting for him. They both went inside the small hut. She heard the door creak shut.

She sat huddled under the rug as the sun slowly disappeared behind a gauze of clouds; she could smell the tang of drying seaweed. The whole world was hushed, except for the whisper of a breeze. There was no way of telling the time except to watch the changing shadows or look out for the turn of the tide. She had woken very early, excited about the sea trip, and now she was tired. After a while her eyes grew heavier... and heavier still. She slept.

❖

Jerking into wakefulness, she staggered to her feet and looked around nervously. *How long has he been gone? When was the sea coming back?* She imagined it lifting the end of the canoe, creeping higher to fill the pools, floating the seaweed, shrinking the chain of islands back into isolated peaks of rock. *What's happened? Have they left me behind?*

She tried to shout but the words were snatched away by a rising wind, lost under the huge sky. 'Where are you?'

Silence for a thudding heartbeat or two. Then she heard his voice, louder than the wind and waves. 'Let's go, then. Go now. We will eat together on the way.' He was talking, but not to her. Then she saw him, and the other man, the lonely king—smiling now, his hat twisted in his hands, her grandfather's arm round his shoulders. They were walking towards her as if returning from a stroll together—coming not over the rocks but from the east, over the open water as if it were dry land, ready for the journey home. ■

PRAYER

Grandfather God, you are patient with us beyond our deserving, gentle beyond our experience, wise beyond our understanding. You reach out to us with compassionate arms, you console us in our loneliness, you seek us out when we are lost and bring us home with you.

57

Prayer through the week

Water

Tony Horsfall is a freelance trainer and retreat leader based in Yorkshire. He is the author of 'Song of the Shepherd' and 'A Fruitful Life', both published by BRF, and writes for 'New Daylight' Bible reading notes.

These prayers are written as meditations on John 4:4–15, where Jesus meets the Samaritan woman at the well at Sychar. The theme of water is prominent in these verses. I have written them in conversational style, with the hope that you will be able to use the words as the basis for your own dialogue with God.

Sunday

When a Samaritan woman came to draw water, Jesus said to her, 'Will you give me a drink?' (John 4:7).

I love this picture of you sitting by the well, Jesus. Seeing you tired from the journey, peckish after an early start, and longing for a cool drink in the midday sun makes you more accessible, more real. It reminds me that you were fully human as well as fully God.

Then I see your vulnerability—not only needing help, but willing to ask for it—and I am aware of my pride and self-sufficiency. Forgive me for my fear of being needy or dependent. When I feel afraid, lonely or just overwhelmed, give me the humility to ask those around me for help, and to call on you, my great high priest.

Monday

The Samaritan woman said to him, 'You are a Jew and I am a Samaritan woman. How can you ask me for a drink?' (For Jews do not associate with Samaritans) (v. 9).

Prejudice is such an ugly sin, Lord, yet it beats in every heart and, I fear, in mine, too. I am so glad that you lived above such pettiness, that you never judge us by the colour of our skin, our gender or our history. I thank you that you see us as unique individuals, made in your image, created to know you, and worth dying for.

I don't know whom I will meet today, Lord, but I pray that I may be open to them with the same non-judgmental love that you have for me. Whatever their race or religion, appearance or manner, may I remember that we share a common humanity—we all know what it is to need a drink of water.

Tuesday

Jesus answered her, 'If you knew the gift of God and who it is that asks you for a drink, you would have asked him and he would have given you living water' (v. 10).

How easy it is to live on the surface of life, Lord, to think that material things are what really matter. Yet every now and then that annoying dissatisfaction creeps in again, and we feel the emptiness and futility of it all once more. The world promises so much, yet never really satisfies.

And now you speak mysteriously of living water. Water that gives life, not just physically, but in a spiritual way. Satisfying, quenching, slaking our thirst for God and for meaning and purpose. Here's my empty cup, Lord. I lift it up for you to fill it yet again.

Wednesday

'Are you greater than our father Jacob, who gave us the well and drank from it himself, as did also his sons and his flocks and herds?' (v. 12).

As I meditate on this little piece of history, I am disturbed, Lord, by some chilling statistics. At this moment 1.1 billion people worldwide lack access to safe, clean water, and 2.4 billion are without basic sanitation. As a result, 2.2 million children under five will die from diarrhoeal diseases this coming year.

What a gift Jacob gave to his people with his well! You who are greater than Jacob know and see this contemporary need, and long to meet it through your people. Today, Lord, I pause to ask that you will empower and enable all who work to improve and develop water supplies, whether as individuals, organizations or communities. Give them success in their labours, I pray. Cause your people to give generously, too, that such help will not be restricted for lack of funds.

Thursday

Jesus answered, 'Everyone who drinks this water will be thirsty again, but those who drink the water I give them will never thirst' (vv. 13–14).

Why does success so often feel hollow, and achievements so empty? Why do relationships break down and true love seem so elusive? Why does the excitement of the latest purchase soon wear off? There seems to be a built-in 'dissatisfaction component' in most of what this world has to offer, Lord. Our souls are always thirsty.

But then, that's how you made us, isn't it? To know you, and therefore to be restless and unfulfilled until we do. It's the thirst that keeps us seeking until we find you, if only we recognize it. Today, Lord, I pray for those important to me—family, friends, colleagues, neighbours who still have this soul thirst—to find for themselves the water of life.

Friday

'Indeed, the water I give them will become in them a spring of water welling up to eternal life' (v. 14).

Here is your answer to our soul-thirst, Lord: our very own portable spring! Your life in mine, your Spirit joined with mine—bubbling over, spilling out and gushing forth with joy and vitality. This is what you intended for us all along. This is eternal life, and we have it now, not just when we die.

Today, Lord, I want to take a few minutes to connect with this spring of life within me. As I sit in your presence, stilled and quieted, I can feel it rising within me. Peace... love... joy.

Your life within me is adequate for whatever challenges I face today. Strength is there. Wisdom is there. Patience is there. Compassion... mercy... forgiveness. It's welling up within me, and I want to set it free, this healing stream!

Saturday

The woman said to him, 'Sir, give me this water so that I won't get thirsty and have to keep coming here to draw water' (v. 15).

I'm not sure about her motives, to be honest, Lord. She doesn't seem to have got the point. I think she wants to avoid the chore of fetching water every day, and I suspect she hasn't really grasped that you are talking about satisfying her soul.

But then, what about my motives? If I'm honest, they are also a bit mixed with self-interest from time to time. Have I really got the point about your message? Perhaps sometimes I read into your words what I want them to mean. At the end of the day, we're all just seekers after the truth, people on a journey trying to understand as best we can.

Thank you for your patience, Lord. Keep speaking to us.

Musings of a middle-aged mystic

Veronica Zundel is a journalist, author and contributor to 'New Daylight'. She has also written 'The Time of Our Lives' for BRF. She lives in north London.

An apocryphal story tells of a man who bought a tree. The seller gave him two small bottles, one with red liquid and one with blue liquid. 'Every morning,' he instructed, 'put one drop of the red liquid into a gallon of water and water the tree. Every evening, put one drop of the blue liquid in a gallon of water and do the same.' The buyer planted the tree, followed the instructions faithfully, and it flourished. The secret, of course, was not in the 'magic' coloured liquids, but in the water!

Water is the stuff of life, and the Bible mentions it frequently, not only as evidence of God's provision for us (Moses striking water from the rock, Exodus 17:6) but also as a symbol of new life (the 'living water' that Jesus promises to the Samaritan woman).

In the UK, clean water is so much a fact of life that we rarely stop to consider it—although recent droughts and hosepipe bans, not to mention water meters, have perhaps made us more aware. It was only when I first visited Israel, however, that the biblical centrality of water really began to make sense to me. You just have to visit the Dead Sea or drive along the Jericho road to appreciate how vital it is to have enough water for crops to grow, or even to graze your goats. Looking at a dry river bed or wadi, it is difficult to imagine that, in the right season, it will be flooded with water and plants will grow all around it.

Perhaps this sort of scene was what Jesus had in mind when he talked of 'living water' or quoted Isaiah 55:1: 'Ho, everyone who thirsts, come to the waters' (NRSV). 'Living water' is, of course, water that moves, washing away debris and cleaning itself as it tumbles over the rocks. On holiday in Austria this year, I experienced this as I drank pure, icy-cold water from a mountain stream (taking good care to drink upstream of the curious cows). The opposite is stagnant water, murky to its depths, covered in algae and insect-haunted.

I have to confess that my life and my faith sometimes feel like a stagnant pond, with a lot of mud at the bottom that I don't care to stir up! Can such a dull body of water be reactivated, purified and made useful for drinking or washing? Experience suggests that it can but, to make it run freely, a lot of debris may need to be cleared away, and a steep rocky path might be a help, too.

At our wedding, by my choice, Ed and I sang the hymn 'Father, hear the prayer we offer', with these lines:

Not for ever by still waters
Would we idly rest and stay
But would smite the living fountains
From the rocks along our way.

Indeed, our path, first battling with infertility and then having a son with an autistic spectrum condition, has had its share of rocks. But there have also been fountains: the miracle of our having a child at all, the joy of finding a church we love. There have been still waters, too: retreats, holidays, opportunities to sit and watch the waves or a gently flowing river or a clear cold lake.

Those who 'delight in the law of the Lord' (Psalm 1) are 'like trees planted by streams of water'. May God's streams never run dry for you. ∎

> **Can such a dull body of water be reactivated?**

> ⌈...clean water is so much a fact of life that we rarely stop to consider it ⌋

Visit the Quiet Spaces website www.quietspaces.org.uk

[Screenshot of www.quietspaces.org.uk website showing navigation: Annual subscriptions, Back issues, Books and resources, Daily Bible reading notes, Quiet days, BRF]

Exploring prayer and spirituality

A new spirituality journal

Time to wonder, to be, to feel, to play, to explore; a pausing point, a breathing space... this three-times-a-year journal is for Christians who are looking for new ways to deepen and develop their faith.

Commendations
Reader comments
Back issues

Now available

Rock
Edited by Naomi Starkey

From trusting in the unchanging, unmoveable rock of our salvation to having faith that can move mountains.

Heather Coupland digs for 'Jewels from the Rock'
Reflections on St Clare of Assisi from Helen Julian CSF
'The Rock in Times of Trouble' - Andrew White

▶ See the full list of contents
▶ Order a copy
▶ Subscribe

Coming Soon

Water (available July 2007)
Edited by Naomi Starkey

Cleansing, cooling, healing, refreshing, life-giving springs...

Joyce Huggett on 'God's gift of water'
Reflections of a Christian surfer from Michael Volland
John Newton's seafaring life of grace

▶ See the full list of contents
▶ Order a copy
▶ Subscribe

We want to hear from you

New site for Quiet Spaces

We have recently upgraded our website. If you find any links that no longer work, please accept our apologies - and we'd be grateful if you could tell us so we can make corrections. Thanks.

Do take a moment to visit the *Quiet Spaces* website (www.quietspaces.org.uk) and email us with your thoughts, perhaps sparked by what you have read in this issue.

In our next issue

Next time we focus on fire, something we enjoy when it offers warmth on a winter's night but fear when a spark ignites a tinder-dry forest. So should we be comforted or terrified when we read that God appeared as a 'pillar of fire' during the exodus? In what ways is our God a fiery God—and what are the implications for us, his children?

Contact us at:

Quiet Spaces,
BRF, First Floor,
Elsfield Hall,
15–17 Elsfield Way,
Oxford OX2 8FG
enquiries@brf.org.uk

QUIET SPACES SUBSCRIPTIONS

Quiet Spaces is published three times a year, in March, July and November. To take out a subscription, please complete this form, indicating the month in which you would like your subscription to begin.

☐ I would like to give a gift subscription (please complete both name and address sections below)

☐ I would like to take out a subscription myself (complete name and address details only once)

This completed coupon should be sent with appropriate payment to BRF. Alternatively, please write to us quoting your name, address, the subscription you would like for either yourself or a friend (with their name and address), the start date and credit card number, expiry date and signature if paying by credit card.

Gift subscription name _____

Gift subscription address _____

_____ Postcode _____

Please send beginning with the next July / November / March issue: *(delete as applicable)*

(please tick box)	UK	SURFACE	AIR MAIL
Quiet Spaces	☐ £16.95	☐ £18.45	☐ £20.85

Please complete the payment details below and send your coupon, with appropriate payment to: BRF, First Floor, Elsfield Hall, 15–17 Elsfield Way, Oxford OX2 8FG.

Name _____

Address _____

_____

Postcode _____ Telephone Number _____

Email _____

☐ Please do not email me any information about BRF publications

Method of payment: ☐ Cheque ☐ Mastercard ☐ Visa ☐ Maestro ☐ Postal Order

Card no. ☐☐☐☐ ☐☐☐☐ ☐☐☐☐ ☐☐☐☐

Valid from ☐☐☐☐ Expires ☐☐☐☐ Issue no. of Maestro card ☐☐

Security Code ☐☐☐

Signature _____ Date ___/___/___

All orders must be accompanied by the appropriate payment.
Please make cheques payable to BRF

PROMO REF: QSWATER

☐ Please do not send me further information about BRF publications

BRF is a Registered Charity